NOTES OF A RAMBLING MAN

THE RAMBLING MAN
A.K.A. THE RAMBLIN' PIRATE

NOTES OF A RAMBLING MAN

THE RAMBLING MAN
A.K.A. THE RAMBLIN' PIRATE

**EDITED & INTRODUCED BY
STEVEN EVETTS**

First published in paperback in 2019 by Sixth Element Publishing
on behalf of Steven Evetts

Arthur Robinson House
13-14 The Green
Billingham TS23 1EU
Tel: 01642 360253
www.6epublishing.net

© Steven Evetts 2019

ISBN 978-1-912218-68-4

British Library Cataloguing in Publication Data. A catalogue record for this book is available from the British Library.

All rights reserved. No part of this publication may be reproduced, stored in a retrieval system or transmitted, in any form or by any means, electronic, mechanical, photocopying, recording and/or otherwise without the prior written permission of the publishers. This book may not be lent, resold, hired out or disposed of by way of trade in any form, binding or cover other than that in which it is published without the prior written consent of the publishers.

Steven Evetts asserts the moral right to be identified as the author of this work.

Printed in Great Britain.

I wanted to list everyone this book was dedicated to.
I realize, despite that being damn near impossible,
I'm fortunate enough that I want to dedicate this
book to so many people that the dedication in itself
could be a book unto its own.

This book is dedicated to every place I have been
and every person I have met, good or bad,
no exception.

CONTENTS

Introduction by *Steven Evetts*...1
Preamble..3

Talking Poems *intro*..7
The Ballad of the Boy from Indianapolis..............................8
Heart Attack Blues 10
Los Angeles *preamble*...12
Los Angeles 13
Haiku Blues...18
Wedding Day 19
Coffee Shop in New York City 21
The Lawman formerly of Topanga Canyon 22
Who Wants to be a Folk Singer?..24
Alaska *story* 26
Alaska 34
Musing #1...36
You Stole My Heart...37
Rambling Pirate..38
Oregon Girl *preamble* 42
Oregon Girl 44
Jorge and Yoel...46
Sitting on My Old Couch Blues...47
Ohio Girl...50
"All we do is Change" or Nothing Stays the Same............52
Franklin Village *preamble*..53
Franklin Village 55
Untitled or 'let the alarm bell ring'.......................................56
Fuck the Grand Canyon 58
Jennifer..59
I've Been Told a Lot of Shit: Part 1 60

Musing #2	63
1969	64
Colors	65
I've Got Options *preamble*	66
I've Got Options	68
Boxer	71
Oh Sweet Jennifer	74
Red, Red Wine	76
I Guess the Lights Went Out in Solana Beach	77
White Russian Table	78
Musing #4	83
I'll Keep on Trying *preamble*	84
I'll Keep on Trying	85
Yellow Bird	87
My Lovesick Confusion Blues *preamble*	90
My Lovesick Confusion Blues	91
Old Friends	93
Rambling #1	94
Grocery Store Blues	95
Musing #5	97
Colorado	98
Old Photographs #1	99
Ye Rustic Inn	100
Russian Girl *story*	102
Russian Girl	107
Trejo's Tacos	108
I've Been Told	109
'Untitled' is the title of this untitled piece titled 'Untitled' *preamble*	110
'Untitled' is the title of this untitled piece titled 'Untitled'	111
For You. From Me	113

Drunk	114
Sometimes	116
Sitting at Home, Writing Alone	117
Harlem *story*	121
Harlem	123
Mr. Bartender Blues	125
27	126
Don't Save Me	127
Good Luck Bar *preamble*	128
Good Luck Bar	130
Unfinished	133
Again and Again	134
Musing #3	136
If I was God for a Day	130
The Black Cat	139
Middlesbrough	140
Goodbye	142
Last Sheet of Paper	145
Talking Poems *outro*	146
Postamble	151

INTRODUCTION

I once knew this writer, he'd occasionally put his words next to the sound of his fingers plucking at guitar strings. Sometimes, they even fit the melody, if that's what you could call it. He wrote this book, or collection of poems mixed with some notes but they had an order, like he meant them to be together, but whether he did or not, they kind of make sense regardless. I've said enough already. I present to you, the notes of a rambling man.

Steven Evetts

PREAMBLE

I have gained
Or been given
Maybe, possibly, earned
The reputation of being a rambling man.
Often shortened to a ramblin' man
Don't worry
Means the same thing.
Throughout some loitering in a shop that offers permanent ink for your skin
It was noted
That I resembled a pirate
So much so, the word pirate was often added in front of my given name
Which progressed and advanced from there, into some sort of
A nickname, I guess
So, in some circles
I became known as the rambling pirate
In other circles, I started to become known as the ramblin' pirate
Don't worry
Doesn't mean anything different.
But it has come to my attention, over the years
That it may possibly be true
True
That I enjoy
From time to time
To ramble on
and
Throughout my rambling

I'll share a few stories
They're as true as I remember
And as false as I care for them to be
I will also deny all knowledge, wherever necessary

Without further ado
I shall do what I do
And before too long
I'll be a ramblin' on

TALKING POEMS *INTRO*

I'm not writing this shit to sound smart
That'll be obvious from the start
I just want to talk
Talk to you
Talking's what I do
I also dig the blues
So there may be some of that too.

These are my talking poems.

Some poems rhyme
Some of them don't
This is one that perhaps does both
I'm not writing to impress
I'm only trying to relieve some stress
The first line rhymed, but this one doesn't, so fuck, I'm doing what I want.

These are my talking poems.

I'll ramble for some time
Maybe cross a few lines
Say what's on my mind
Treasure we may find
Some sentence that ends with the word kind
I just want to talk
Talking's what I do
These are my talking poems and I hope they talk to you.

THE BALLAD OF THE BOY FROM INDIANAPOLIS

You were just a kid when you got locked up by the law
Nine years for robbing a grocery store
Told 'em you were coming out the meanest bastard
they ever saw
And Johnny, they ain't seen anyone like you ever before.

You took down your first bank before too long
Probably celebrated that night, I imagine a cabaret,
with some jazz songs
But I'm only guessing y'know, I could be wrong
But soon the police would come along.

I'm sure you felt you'd done all you can
They couldn't figure out the note on the paper,
they had no idea man.
But they'd soon witness, your genius escape plan
As you'd walk out of Lima with the rest of your gang.

No prison walls could keep you inside
Laid low amongst the public, they were on your side.
You were a kind of Robin Hood, or at least you tried.
I think Evelyn was in love, she even helped you hide
when you needed to.

They waited for the movie to end, to see the girl in red
She was actually in orange, but red sounds better,
at least that is what the press said
Outside the Biograph, is where they pronounced you dead
People dipped handkerchiefs, on the parts of the street
that you bled.

I did hear you hadn't been looking how you used to do
And that there was a guy in town, that was supposed to
look a lot like you
Some say that maybe that wasn't you, and maybe,
you made it through
I don't know about all that…

but would be cool if it was true.

HEART ATTACK BLUES

He had the heroin blues
A needle and a spoon
Lost to whatever tune
Was playing that day.
The heart attack blues.

She had the cocaine twitch
And the allergy itch
She was rocking that bitch
There was some partying that day.
The heart attack blues.

He had the fast food love
The Big Mac from above
Two of them, one's not enough
He had some food that day.
The heart attack blues.

She was teaching those kids
The cracks of society they slid
As they say "God forbid"
She was teaching their hope that day.
The heart attack blues.

He was on his five-mile run
Thought he'd run an extra one for fun
All of a sudden, he was done
When he went for a run that day.
The heart attack blues.

She was eating pancakes
I mean pancakes, for fuck's sake
Fair enough, she was baked
At least things were tasting good that day.
The heart attack blues.

He was on his twelfth pint
The night being out of sight
Sadly, no cigarette for his light
On that drunken day.
The heart attack blues.

She was deciding who to let go
There's a recession you know
Before they opened that door
She was no more. On the firing day.
The heart attack blues.

He sat naked when he took the pill
She was waiting to give into his will
A smile on their faces when he fell still
At least they were happy on that final day.
The heart attack blues.

LOS ANGELES *PREAMBLE*

It struck me, I've been lucky enough to travel a few places,

some I stayed longer than others.

For me to be writing these words to you now,

means those places that I've been to,

I've also come from

and I've always been treated okay.

I spent a good few years in

Los Angeles.

I suppose, this is my thank you, to you.

LOS ANGELES

Had my first roommates,
I swear they were great.
I was eighteen years old for fuck's sake,
Made a lot of mistakes.

I was looked after in Los Angeles.

I didn't know where I was sleeping for certain
Crashed in your living room, you put up a curtain,
A sleeping bag on the floor, was pretty rough
Stayed there six months.

I was looked after in Los Angeles.

You said I could crash in your loft
The air mattress was pretty soft
It was a nice place, couldn't ask for more
Perez Hilton apparently lived next door.
*(I didn't know who he was but he's some sort of media guy
and I did know he was making more money than me, thus,
highlighting the point I should not have been staying in such
an establishment as this. I mean, I had to sneak past the security
guard at the gate every night, till he got to know me that is,
then he'd let me in).*

I was looked after in Los Angeles.

I was staying at Hoover and 12th
When these guys threatened my health
I slept on a couch in Los Feliz,
Up there, much more peace

I was looked after in Los Angeles.

There was this guy on the bus
He was looking kind of rough
I was so tired, I dozed off
He tapped me on the shoulder before my stop

I was looked after in Los Angeles.

I was thinking about going home
You told me I wasn't alone
That I could stay with you
Didn't realize we'd fall in love too.

I was looked after in Los Angeles.

When we weren't getting married anymore
I slept on my friend's floor,
There was five of us in a studio
Studios are built for one you know

I was looked after in Los Angeles.

I found out my Grandad passed away,
I called in work to say,
I wouldn't be making it in that day
They said "Don't have to come in tomorrow."
I said "I'll be okay"

I was looked after in Los Angeles.

I was totally broke
Really hoping to smoke.
Made a call and in a jiff
We were sat smoking a spliff

I was looked after in Los Angeles.

I was dating this girl
I mean, she meant the world
It didn't work out
So, we went downtown.

I was looked after in Los Angeles.

I order coffee at the café
Hostess asks if I'm okay
Said I hadn't eaten today
She gave me free pastries

I was looked after in Los Angeles.

We went to drink some beer
Make our heads go clear
We order a bunch of drinks
Bartender charges us for six
(We ordered eight shots of whiskey four bottles of beer, I'm no math major, but I know, that, is more than six drinks)

I was looked after in Los Angeles.

There was a place on Vine, helped straighten me out
Couldn't write this thing, without giving them a shout
I'm riding the storm out here, it's cold on this route.
I'll stop by, when I'm next about.

I was looked after in Los Angeles.

There was this tattoo shop
Over in West Hollywood
They tattooed me a lot
Shit, I lived in that shop.

I was looked after in Los Angeles.

There was a girl with a cat
Her place she'd let me crash
When I had no place to go.
Spent too long with no address don't you know.

I was looked after in Los Angeles.

The bar I worked in has closed
What to do next? I didn't know.
I was recommended this place
Started working down in Venice.

I was looked after in Los Angeles.

I just heard that my friend had died
Those emotions are hard to hide
Heroin man, it's a hell of a drug
My boss asks if I want to get drunk.

I was looked after in Los Angeles.

We were walking by the Greek
Violent Femmes were playing, so we tried to sneak a peak
The ticket lady shouts over "you guys want to see?
Come here I'll let you see for free"

I was looked after in Los Angeles.

When I was crying on the floor a broken shell of a man
I had an empty bottle in my hand
You came over that day
Told me everything was going to be okay

I was looked after in Los Angeles.

We were hiking near Murphy's Ranch
Off the beaten path
Lost my footing and I nearly collapsed
But I was saved by some flimsy ass tree branch

I was looked after in Los Angeles.

I was on a thirty-hour train ride
I was certainly ready to get a little high
My friend he picked me up at Union Station
He had a joint there for me waiting

I was looked after in Los Angeles.

HAIKU BLUES

i got haiku blues

like Elvis's blue suede shoes

the blues like haikus

WEDDING DAY

My glass is empty
But in the bottle, there's plenty
I'm thinking about us, in our early twenties

My head was a mess

And I let you go
I should have known
Someone else, was going to steal the show

At the time, it might not have made sense

But, I always thought I'd be there
I never ceased to care
Even if I never made you aware

But I did what I thought was best

It simply wouldn't be true
If I said, I never thought about standing next to you
Taking your hand and saying "I do"

I understand. I mean, I failed every test.

Cigarette ash resting on my shoe
Me and him never saw eye to eye,
but I know he loves you too
I suppose, some days, are just for getting through

I couldn't love you more, I couldn't hate you less

I'm still looking for romance
Drunk again in this bar, taking my chance
While the two of you, are sharing your first dance

Goddamn, I guess I'm still a mess

I wish I was there, in every way
Even if it was only to say
You always deserved, the greatest wedding day.

COFFEE SHOP IN NEW YORK CITY

We were sitting in a coffee shop, in old New York City

Looking out at Morningside Park, oh so pretty

This old timer came in and sat down with his tea

Decided to sit right on down next to me

Told me he was Hungarian,

then shared some more of his ancestry

He came to America after fleeing the country

He spent eight months in a Yugoslavian concentration camp you see

He said they were the best eight months of his life,

I said "they couldn't be"

He said "I'll tell you why my son, they really set me free"

Said, "how many kids get the chance at twenty-three

To plan the rest of their lives in solitary?"

He said everything he planned, he has done,

Now they're just memories.

THE LAWMAN FORMERLY OF TOPANGA CANYON

The lawman said
He'd put a bullet in my head
If I came into his town again.
You see, there was a girl
I mean there's always a girl, but to me,
she really meant the world
The problem was
The self-made lawman, had always longed for her
He'd seen her grow from sixteen years old
Watched her become a woman
When I first met her, she was already there
But we fell in love
The kind of falling where it's never enough
Sure, he was jealous, but he took it pretty well
Even became friends, that was until
He pulled out that gun
And told me to run
Some kind of lawman…
I suppose there's one in every town.
He used to live up in Topanga, owned a lion
he'd been kicked out of every bar without trying
he was a law unto his own, a one-man team
keeping the streets, his kind of clean
if you know what I mean
He reckoned, it was the looks he lacked
And rambled to me about Cyrano de Bergerac
But this story isn't finished
as mine and the lawman's friendship diminished.
I told him I wasn't going to be around
He said, if I left, I should never come back to his town

Said, there'd be a bullet for me waiting around
My name on it
I didn't give a shit
I was heartbroken.
You see, me and this girl had fallen too far
Too much love to handle, too much hate to hold
We both took it pretty hard
But she didn't want anyone to be told
Especially the lawman
she wanted to tell him herself
Didn't want him to get the wrong idea
She wanted to be crystal clear
Well, I wished you'd talked to him sooner dear,
because he was pretty damned clear when he
placed the gun near my ear
And told me to leave.
Before the bullet he promised, refused to wait
I wasn't prepared to hesitate
He said he'd be waiting
If I ever went back to that place.

I eventually went back… but I left it a few days.

WHO WANTS TO BE A FOLK SINGER?

There was a man, he worked with his hands, picking
guitar strings of course,
He'd sing in the morn, ramble past dawn,
till his voice became hoarse.
Off stage he was known to stumble, always humble,
with a beer in his hand,
Shows every night, his fingers weren't right,
so he joined a jam band, man.
A few tabs of acid to keep him placid,
late to a gig in Los Angeles.

There was a woman, she worked with her hands,
picking guitar strings of course,
She'd sing all the time, creating her rhymes,
till her voice became hoarse.
Her daddy was a moonshiner, a taste no finer,
till he was taken to the station.
He played strings man, upright bass in the prison band,
during his incarceration.
A few shots of tequila, got her kind of feeling,
ready for her gig in Los Angeles.

There was a dog, did not work with his hands,
no picking guitar strings of course,
The dog would bark between songs and during
try to sing along, till his voice became hoarse.
Every folk singer that comes to town likes to have
a dog around, I'm not quite sure why.
I think it's safe to assume, when they hot boxed the room
the dog received a second hand high.

A bandana on its collar, onstage he follows,
ready for the gig in Los Angeles.

Give a folk singer a guitar they'll write you a song.

Give a folk singer an apple they'll make you a bong.

ALASKA *STORY*

I lived in this apartment, I mean, if you could call it that.
I could open the front door without getting out of bed,
you know,
one of those shoebox type places.
I only had to leave my bed to piss, and that's only
because the toilet was around the corner,
And, well, I'm not that talented.
But, it was my place.
Had a few cockroaches too,
the big outside ones.
I lived on the ground floor.
Swear to God, I walked into my place one day and I
thought I got the wrong apartment, there was about
three of them,
lounging, watching tv, bowls of popcorn and shit.
I swear they were big,
I knew they were big when one of them was wearing
my t shirt and it was too small for him.
Anyway, this place was East Hollywood/Los Feliz area.
Los Feliz area,
nice.
It has hills, big houses and shit, they were north of
my block.
South of my block,
East Hollywood,
I don't want to say not as nice because I had some
good times over there,
but I did hear the police call that stretch 'crime corridor'
because, well,
it's a corridor of crime.

My particular apartment was located in the southern
portion of my block.
My friend lived in the building next to mine,
same management, different buildings,
but same deal.
To make a short story longer,
we were hanging out one day and he was planning to head
back to Alaska for a month,
said I should come visit.
Ladies and gentlemen,
I do not need much persuading to go anywhere,
Especially, when I got a place to crash,
which he told me I did.
I said I'd fly out with him
stay a few days,
because he's not too keen on the flying thing.
I don't like it,
but, man,
he really doesn't like it.
Before we flew out I did my usual pre-flight routine
Drink a beer, smoke a few joints, take an ibuprofen
(I get migraines when I fly sometimes) I take an edible
right before security then head to the bar.
He did not induldge with me,
and let me tell you,
I was far more relaxed,
I ain't saying it's good for you,
but, shit,
works for me.
We drink a few Bloody Marys,
the first two are for the flight,
the third is to forget the cost of the Bloody Marys,

at an airport bar,
particularly,
LAX.
We drank a couple during the flight,
made it to the bar on our layover in Seattle
before we drank a couple more on the next flight.
So, needless to say,
we arrived in somewhat of a state of intoxication.
We had some food got settled in.
Drank a few more on the decking.
Next day.
Wake up.
I'm told we're going on a hike,
I was thinking more of a slow hungover walk,
hit up my friends weed contacts and go stare at a
mountain or some shit.
But, no,
weather was good.
Apparently when the weather is good,
you gotta do stuff.
So, my friend, his sister and I,
make our way to the start of this trail,
has this sign of all the shit you need,
like water, maps, headlamps and shit.
Swear to God,
I had a can of soda,
a pack of smokes
and a half-eaten candy bar.
We set off,
I'm not gonna lie,
I don't like heights,
I try not to let that stop me, but let me tell you this,

we hiked so high
I could see the top of airplanes,
they were flying beneath us.
I'm no genius,
But, that is higher than I need to be.
We eventually make it to the top,
That is the moment my friend tells me we just hiked
Mount Juneau,
The tallest fucking mountain in Juneau.
I am not averse to walking outside
But, I am no hiker.
Walking is a means to get to a place,
if that place is hard to get to,
I'll do it
But, if I'm hiking a mountain
I like a little warning.
It was beautiful, but, I did not enjoy coming down,
because the height is much more noticeable,
on the way down.
There, is this lift so far up the mountain,
It ferries people from the base to the bar and restaurant,
or gives people a head start on their hikes.
I was told about this lift after the fact.
By this lift was the bar,
and let me tell you,
it was one of the nicest beers of my life.
We have ourselves a few beverages when we got back,
and our bodies ached.
They fucking really ached.
I could barely move, man.
Next morning,
I wake up

I'm told we're going to see some ice caves,
only problem,
you can't drive to them.
You have to hike.
I thought to myself
"hell no",
I asked how much of a hike,
he said a few hours.
I thought "fuck no"
then his sister came in,
she said
"hell no".
I said
"that's a shame"
So, he called his friend
and his friend said
"no problem, we can still go, I'll just get us some kayaks"
I look to my friend's sister
as if to say, hell no right?
but she says
"sure, as long as I don't have to use my legs."
I'm thinking,
I am in pain
and my friend's guy with the pain relief medication
has not shown up yet.
Weed's legal in Alaska
but they had no shops in the area.
I know I saw a mountain the day before
but climbing a mountain is much different
to smoking a joint and staring at one.
So, we drove out to pick up the kayaks,
we drag them to the water.

I should mention,
I am not a kayaker.
Anyway,
there is me, not a kayaker
my friend's sister, not a kayaker
my friend, not necessarily a kayaker
but he seemed he had what it took to become one.
His friend goddamn Kayak Joe,
whom is now my friend, I like to think,
but Kayak and his girlfriend, both experienced in the art of the kayak.
I see these things that are apparently called 'skirts',
I ask Kayak Joe if we need them,
I was told we did not. It was optional.
I thought
well, shit,
if no one else is using these skirt things
I won't use one.
Mistake.
We hit the water,
first twenty minutes,
great,
laughter, smiles, jokes, overtaking, undertaking, water calm, not a wave in sight.
We turn the corner
and let's just say
we found all the waves that were not there before.
We all separated,
Kayak Joe and his girlfriend are fucking gone.
They thought fuck these waves let's use our abilities to get out the water
I hung back with my friend and his sister,

in some grandiose gesture of solidarity.
The waves began to come over the front
and we started crashing into each other.
As we push into the waves,
it dawns on me in that moment,
I was,
in absolutely no way
helping the situation.
I wanted to help,
but I had become a hindrance.
So, I decided to speed off,
in order to get out of those waves,
as quickly as I could.
Kayak Joe was telling me how to come to shore.
He came out to pull me in
but I was too busy taking my shoes off.
So, I'd have something to throw at him.
Sure, it was cold
But my shoes were too wet to be useful
My friend and his sister also made it in
But they kept their shoes on
and I was soaked
head to toe
but,
The ice caves
man
they were a trip
I was soaked.
But they were a trip.
I'd never seen anything like it.
The way back was easier
because the waves did the work

and I was already part ocean.
In fact,
I may have been wetter than the ocean.
We make it to shore,
and start dragging our equipment to the car,
I see a couple of dirty looking old timers
drinking some beers.
I was told to leave them alone,
but, they started talking to me.
My friends left me alone,
They didn't want to know,
but I still have this couple's number in my phone,
and let's just say,
before we got back to the car,
the cigarette they gave me started kicking in,
and on that drive back
well, on the drive back
the mountains were looking pretty damn cool
this next piece is for everyone and everything that took care of me in Alaska.

ALASKA

We made our way through the snow
As we hiked on up Mount Juneau
Had a pack of smokes and a can of coke
I was underprepared for that hike, no joke.

I was looked after in Alaska.

Water was calm there were no waves
As we kayaked to the ice caves
Then we turned the corner, I will never forget
Water was not calm, lots of waves, got wet.

I was looked after in Alaska.

Walking to yours there were no cabs
We had won a couple of hundred on some pull tabs
Barely walking in a straight line
We both thought we could pull down that road sign…
We could not.

I was looked after in Alaska.

Walking on the beach that night
Maybe this fire will just light
Away from all the bricks and mortar
I can hear the salmon in the water.

I was looked after in Alaska.

We made our way into town
Went to every bar we found
We were looking for food if we could find any
That's when you introduced me to pelmeni…
Game Changer… Delicious.

I was looked after in Alaska.

MUSING #1

From start to finish

You were in the race

Hopes diminished

But you won just in case.

YOU STOLE MY HEART

It's strange to think about
And even stranger to say aloud
But baby, I'm stepping out
A man can only be so proud
I've lost my voice too much to shout
It's clear you don't want me around.

So, into the night I will go
I know when it's time to hit the road
I should have gone a while ago, I know
I was hoping you'd help me carry this load
But it's time to cancel the show
Don't worry, it's nowhere I haven't been before.

Its wild out there, but I'll do fine
Sometimes it comes easy, sometimes it's a grind
I'll get by without you being mine,
I guess if I'm not yours, I won't mind.
Maybe all we need is time,
but who knows out here what we'll find.

RAMBLING PIRATE

I'm a goddamn rambling man

Ramble every time I can

I'm a keep on being the same old rambler

Whiskey drinker and gambler

They call me the rambling pirate

'Cos I walk sideways when I'm on the rum diet

I'm not saying you have to buy it

But I ain't lying I'm the rambling pirate

So, come sail the seas with me

Out on the water we'll forever be free

Setting sail for wherever we want to be

Living our life of leisure

Soaking up inside our own pleasure

Maybe write a few stories, find a few treasures

When our money gets low

I'll find us some place to go

I am a rambling pirate after all

When we get to whichever place

We can stay there, a few days

But we should warn them anyways

Pirates can make people feel many ways

So just in case, lock up your daughters

Hide the jewels you bought her

The Rambling Pirate is around

People generally don't like pirates in their town

Especially not rambling ones

They may not loot the local store

But we ramble on like you never heard before

Sometimes it won't make sense

You may even take offense

But by some stroke of luck

This rambling pirate has more than a book

More than these shoes covered in muck

I've also mastered the art of not giving a fuck.

OREGON GIRL *PREAMBLE*

I'd been up to Oregon a few of times
Both with friends and alone
There was a friend of mine I knew from another friend
Rumor has it,
he once drank a bottle of bourbon
resulting in him confusing 6pm for 6am
on a camping adventure
I wasn't there but my friend from Alaska
Liked to recall the story
Quite often
Normally when drinking at Ye Rustic
Where we all liked to go.
This friend had moved up North
He said I could crash at his for a few days
The first night we had a few in his local
Place had a pool table
Dartboard
And one of those Big Buck Hunter games
In fact,
In some classic barroom mix-up
One of the other patrons
Played our dollar on that very game
Shit, he seemed so happy
I wasn't even mad
Anyway, the next night came
And my friend was unavailable
I had a gig to get to
Before the show,
I did
What I do

Most shows
I arrive early,
I scout the local bars
Maybe have a drink or two
Do the whole 'show' thing
Then return to whichever was the preferred bar
Normally it is not the closest bar to the venue
But sometimes there is little choice
This particular time
I found a bar a few minutes walk away
from the Aladdin Theater
It was in this particular bar
I got to talking
And this next piece is about
The person I got talking to.

OREGON GIRL

We met in that old rundown bar
It was long after dark
There was nowhere to sit
I saw you smoking a cigarette
Your friends were leaving, but you decided to stay
I still remember it like it was yesterday
It was getting pretty late
And I was no longer walking straight
We drank till last orders
You spoke about your daughter
And your hope for brighter days ahead
Kept going to the bathroom, suppose a habit
needs to be fed
We staggered onto that Portland street
Both trying to keep our feet
I guess we were both pretty trashed
But you led me round the corner,
to find the joint you stashed
You asked if I wanted to go for a walk
Showed me your favorite place, where we sat and talked
You could see the whole city on top of that hill
The sun was rising and the leaves were still
I'll always remember that kiss
It was our first and last but still a kiss I miss
I walked you to your door
Knowing we wouldn't see each other anymore
You managed to get in touch a few months ago
It was really good hearing from you, truth be told
Seems you're no longer drinking from that old loving cup
And things have really started looking up

The past always tends to unfurl
Keep on, keeping on my Oregon girl.

JORGE AND YOEL

Now, I'm not attempting to be rude
They always said you were a bad ass dude
And your good friend was too
You and him, were down South America way
Taking a break from the amount that you train
Like two lions that a cage is trying to tame
That's what brought you some fame
At least enough for the club to comp your bill
That was at least until
You finished the second bottle and asked for a refill
Then came the end of the night
You were certainly feeling alright
That was until the server came over and said
"you know the tab's not paid right?"
They should have known you guys weren't
the ones to fight
Ten thousand is what they wanted you to pay
Of course, you said "no damn way
you told us we were getting comped today"
They said it was written down in the print real fine
So, cough up your money and don't step out of line
You left that night without giving them a dime
They were no match for you guys at any time

Because you are two badass motherfuckers.

SITTING ON MY OLD COUCH BLUES

I was looking for a box of notebooks in my storage unit

Had to move to a new place and none of this fit

I saw my old couch in the corner, so I decided to sit

This old lady had been with me for a bit

If it could talk it would probably say a lot of shit

Maybe it would ask a lot of questions

Like:

Why the hell did you steal that road sign?

Why did you tell her you were doing fine?

Then when she left you made me watch Blue Valentine

(Good movie but you know… it's a little bleak)

Why did you and her drink all that wine?

Why would you always drink yourself blind?

Why are you always looking for whatever trouble you could find?

Why were you always trying to make your words rhyme?

Why were you howling at the moon so many times?

I don't really know what you're supposed to do

When you've got the sitting on your old couch blues.

Wonder what it would say about all the faces it's seen?

Like:

Why was the girl with the eyeliner so keen?

Why was that dude in the suit acting so mean?

Why was the girl with the bandana acting so free?

Why was that guy smoking that stuff talking to me?

Who was that dude wearing shorts that tried to head-butt the tv?

Why were you and your friends always playing your music so loudly?

She was here all the time, but for a while I haven't seen

I miss her too. Where has she been?

I miss you two holding hands on top of me.

Well I don't know about you

But I got the sitting on my old couch blues

Now my couch friend, I have to tell you a thing or two.

Life is easier as a couch, I mean, people tend
to come to you

In real life people don't tend to come around so easy

If they do they don't tend to stick around so easy,
believe me.

I got the sitting on my old couch blues.

OHIO GIRL

I was sitting in one of those twelve step rooms
I'd been going there a year or two
It wasn't great, but I was pulling through
It was all worth it, when I met you
You sat across from me
Looking like there was anywhere you'd rather be
They asked for your name
But you had nothing to say
You just sat silently
After the serenity prayer
You were no longer there
So, I looked outside
I knew you were trying to hide
But I'd regret it if I didn't try
Sure, I was completely smitten
But those rooms have rules, not all of them written
But this one made some kind of sense,
unlike some of the others
It's best not to turn newcomers into lovers
But I just wanted to let you know
As cliché as it sounded
You were not alone
I can be on the end of any telephone
I was celebrating a friend's birthday
When you called me up to say
Things were not okay
We talked most of that night
Out on your roof soaking in the moonlight
Still seemed pretty dark.
I sat with you a few times while you were drinking

I wonder, what you must have been thinking
But all of a sudden without a hitch
It seemed like everything finally clicked
I mean, shit, it's been a few years now.
So, I suppose, as the story goes
I became your eskimo
And I just want you to know
It was me alone, that decided to step out into the cold
Lately, I've been doing alright
But I'm back sitting in the moonlight
Wondering which of my decisions were right
I know, I could have kissed you, and I often wish that I did
But normally, when I kiss someone, it all turns to shit
It took more for you to quit
Than for me to start again
Who knows, maybe our path will eventually
come together, my friend.

"ALL WE DO IS CHANGE" OR NOTHING STAYS THE SAME

A guy once said "All we do is change"
I say, nothing stays the same
Just the memories remain
I think I'm out of range
Of letting this cycle move on
But I'm listening to this song
He's singing "all we do is change"
This is just a phase
Well I've moved about a lot
Still landing in the same old place
But I'm hoping that
That too, is a phase
'Cos I'm slowly going insane
from everything feeling the same
I guess I used to want to leave a legacy
Now I don't know if I want anyone to remember me
Thought it was holding me back
Maybe it set me free
I guess nothing stays the same
It can't, if "all we do is change"
I can still feel the pain
But I'm not crying on the floor today
Even got a smile on my face
I suppose we all go different ways
Honey, everything will be okay
Has to be
Because nothing stays the same
And "all we do is change".

FRANKLIN VILLAGE *PREAMBLE*

Franklin Village
Is this village in Hollywood
At the foot of the hills
Which basically means
They charge you a dollar more for coffee
It also means there's a bunch of people
drinking kale and shit
One time me and my friend walked by with a crate of PBR,
a bottle of bourbon, a large pizza and two bags of chips.
I swear to God,
People stopped us in the street
Like celebrities
Anyway,
The village consists of residential areas and all that jazz
But essentially
Franklin Village is a block
A magazine stand
A clothes store
A sushi place
Two coffee shops
And
Three bars
(the sushi place also serves alcohol, but it's not a bar let's
be honest, last thing you need to see at a bar is raw fish)
and then there is UCB
an improv comedy joint
there's always a line down the street
the only people that like this line
are the people in this line
and even some of them, never seem too pleased

depends on the show
One of the coffee shops
Was open till four in the morning
Had a pool table
Depending who was working
They may even give me the keys
Sometimes food cost ten bucks
Sometimes it was free
Suicide Girls had the place upstairs
Don't know if they still do
But I always thought that was pretty cool
If I longed for a stronger libation
There was three options
They would vary in price
But the Happy Hours were all at different times
So, we'd hit all three
End up wherever the drunk wanted us to be
I had some good times
Had some rough ones too
That street could share a story or two
Some stories I can't write
Because I don't remember a fucking thing
But what I do know
Is I made some friends for life
I'd been at my best
I'd been at my worst

It's been a while

You're far from perfect
But, I kind of love your flaws.

Franklin Village, these are my words for you.

FRANKLIN VILLAGE

My feet they staggered,
As I start to feel a bit haggard
But, the sun keeps shining
And I'm not particularly minding
On my walk to Franklin Village.

I walk past the fruit stand
Making my way across 'hobo island'
Taking a right on Edgemont
Going whichever way I want
On my walk to Franklin Village.

I stop by the gas station,
Pick up water for hydration
And two packs of smokes
'cos Village prices are a joke
On my walk to Franklin Village.

The coffee shop on the corner
Iced coffee is my first order
I look to see who's around
Immediately familiar faces are found
During my time in Franklin Village.

I walk the whole block
While my friends sit and talk
A cigarette in my hand
I check out the magazine stand
During my time in Franklin Village.

It's time to hit all three bars
Friends at each, swallowing jars
The bars tell us it's time to go
Now commences the sidewalk show
During my time in Franklin Village.

My friends and I walk along
Singing the occasional song
Not ready to go
We head to the joint open till four
On my walk from Franklin Village.

We enter this Thai place
They seem to know my face
One friend looks a bit ropey
As he signs himself up for karaoke
On my walk from Franklin Village.

They've stopped serving drinks
What do you guys think?
Should we head our separate ways?
I guess we're heading to my place
On our walk from Franklin Village.

UNTITLED OR 'LET THE ALARM BELL RING'

I turned and you were there
Smiling back at me
But dreams they hurt
And happen so casually.

The alarm it rang, I let it ring
There's no call to go outside
The alarm still rings, how it rings
But time just passes by.

I turned and you were gone
Emptiness filled the space
Until I became a song
Only, my melody was late.

The phone it rang, I let it ring
There's no need to pick up words
The phone it rings, how it rings
Your voice is sweeter when it hurts.

I turned and you were there
But only as a memory
I suppose, that's what I must learn to prefer
At least that's what they keep telling me.

FUCK THE GRAND CANYON

We were driving through Arizona
Thought we'd check out the Grand Canyon
I'd be lying if I told you
That the view was the best part of the day
Yeah, sure, the view was great
But, on our way out, we stopped at this burger place
Burger was so damn good, I can still taste it
But this story doesn't have a happy ending I'm afraid.
The world's best burger and I can't remember the
name of the place.
Is it even still there?
Moved to a new place? Could be anywhere.
I swear, you're there, every time I close my eyes.
I even turned vegan for a while.
If I were ever in Arizona again I'll search for that
joint and get that burger,
In fact, I'd get two or three, just leave the fries
This is not a dream that will ever be realized, of course.
Maybe it wouldn't be as good or maybe it's just the same.
Either way I'll never know, because I still can't
remember its name.

Fuck the Grand Canyon. Makes me think about a burger
I'll never have again.

JENNIFER

You were so forward
and I was so awkward
didn't know what to say.
I'd been sad for a while
aching bad for a smile
didn't know what to say, that day.
I said "I hope you understand."
You took me by the hand
told me everything was going to be okay.
I didn't really buy it
but you did make everything quiet
that day over at San Francisco Bay.
Didn't know what I was doing that night
you were too sweet for anything to feel right
you were bright yellow and I'd turned grey.
On the road, I must travel
before everything unravels
and you won't talk to me again.
Next time I'm in town
I'll see if you're around
'cos y'know nothing stays the same.

We all grow with age.
That won't change.

I'VE BEEN TOLD A LOT OF SHIT: PART 1

When I was a kid
I was told the color blue was blue
Told one plus one is what it took to make two
A joey is a baby kangaroo
But I was also told,
The Book of Mormon was true
And church was just a thing we had to do
Cut me some slack guys, I also believed in Santa Claus too, didn't you?

Yes, it's weird being raised Mormon.

They say there's these temples you have to visit
You get baptized for dead people in it
They say they baptized Anne Frank, ain't that some shit.
Not allowed alcohol, not even a bit.
Can't show your shoulders, must wear sleeves
Joseph Smith saw God hanging out by some trees.
I know this shit sounds crazy
Like when you talk to God you must be on your knees
I saw a tape like that once it was starring Ron Jeremy
I mean there's a lot of shit that they say
Like it's not okay to get married when you're gay
But if you pray real hard, those feelings may go away
If they don't, no worries just don't act on them okay?
Like I said man, they say a lot of crazy shit.

I once quoted Malcolm X in church
That must have scared them as they believe
black skin is a curse

Yeah, they deny it now, but it's still written in the verse
And don't think that book is free, they will take
ten percent of your purse
Those temples don't build themselves y'know
When I left, I suddenly felt freed
Because, there's a bunch of contradictions I could no
longer believe
Like it says in the bible go forth and spread your seed
But Mormons say no sex before you're married.
Which is okay for old Jo' Smith, shit,
he lost count of his wives.

Man, you're told a lot of shit when you're raised Mormon

Like:
They said the Israelites got lost in America
twelve groups became tribal
If you are dancing with a girl you must make sure
there is space between you to fit a bible,
To live with a woman you have to wait
In the meantime you absolutely cannot masturbate
They told me I needed to cut my hair
Otherwise they wouldn't let me wear the magic underwear
They used to say you could have more than one wife
Also said if you have a disability you were probably
naughty before this life.

Man, I'm glad I left that shit when I was twenty-one
It absolutely had to be done
I'm only sorry that it took so long
And that I had to be an adult.
Before I finally left the cult.

I say cult, cos well, shit, if a Mormon and a Scientologist met in a bar they'd probably get along, I mean only because you shouldn't really talk on religion or politics at a bar.

MUSING #2

I don't fucking like marmite

Actually I fucking might.

I fucking might like marmite.

They said it wouldn't happen.

Bunch of fucking idiots.

1969

Hippies were all peace and free love, until you came along
Singing your "People say I'm no good" song
All that pain over a couple of summer nights
Maybe the people you sang about were right
You knew you were no good at all
It's written in blood, dripping on the wall
So many lives will never be the same again
Suppose, they were looking for family
and found the worst of men
Bringing to earth the most violent hell
Damning themselves to viewing life from a cell
Teenagers with everything to live for
Didn't know they were selling their souls

I'm driving down Waverly Drive
Thinking about Cielo Drive
People will probably remember how they died
But in the heart of Hollywood they're still alive.

COLORS

The sky is pretty clear
A few clouds scattered here and there
Can feel the sand beneath my feet
Take a seat,
We'll stay the night
The sun will be setting soon
Should be quite the sight to see
Also hear it's a full moon.
We can head to the pier
Check out the lights
We'll stay here tonight.

But I gotta tell you something baby,
And you may not care
But I swear
I haven't seen colors for fucking years.
Ever since you first left
I became melody deaf
I'm glad that you're back
But it's only just that
The food's still a waste
Because I still can't taste
I haven't seen colors in fucking years.
Every time I'm touched
I still don't feel very much.
I know we're together now
But my senses haven't come back somehow
Some people say
All they see is grey
I don't even see grey there
I haven't seen colors in fucking years.

I'VE GOT OPTIONS *PREAMBLE*

This next one,

is about,

the friend,

the friend you develop feelings for,

if that's ever happened to you,

it can quickly become a complex situation.

There was this one girl,

I talked to her all the time,

We would hang out for hours,

Our friends could be asleep around us,

We'd talk till the sun rose.

All of a sudden,

She was "busy"

When someone is busy enough,

It can seem like you have nothing to do,

I thought about asking her to hang out,

Instead,

I wrote this...

I'VE GOT OPTIONS

So, you don't want to see me?
Well, I don't want to see you
I know I kissed you, or you kissed me
You see, you told me, I don't belong to you
So, baby I'll do what I want to do,
With or without you, unless you want to do
Something with me, then baby I'm free.
But if you don't want to see me
I got better things to do
And now I don't want to see you
You're asking me what things I might do.

There's a movie I want to see
I don't really have the money
And movie theatres aren't free.

I could always head to the bar
But then my friend would come and he'd bring his car
That for me is a bit too far
I could tell that friend I'm staying home, then to the bar
I go, but he drives there every night regardless. I'm just
trying to say I got options.

I hear there's a coffee shop open till late
Maybe I'll take a girl on a coffee date
Y'know drink some coffee play around with fate

Oh baby, I have a song in my heart
I could stay home and give the lyrics a start
Or I could respond to my friend's message
about Mario Kart

For the record I don't play Mario Kart, I maybe done it once, I lost, crashed a lot. Came last. I'm just trying to say baby I have options.

I could go to the pool hall
Could win some money after all
Depending who's there, chances are probably small.

I could go to the Grove
Buy some expensive ass clothes
Maybe even an iphone
I know I'm broke and think technology's a joke
but I'm just saying baby I got options.

So you don't want to see me?
Well, I don't want to see you
I know I kissed you, or you kissed me
You see, you told me, I don't belong to you
So baby I'll do what I want to do,
With or without you, unless you want to do
Something with me then baby I'm free.
But if you don't want to see me
I got better things to do
And now I don't want to see you
You're asking me what things I might do.

I could take a friend to dinner
Sushi happy hour always a winner
Plus, you said I was looking thinner.

I could go to that pottery class
I always said it'd be a laugh
But you wouldn't go cos I'm "a pain in the ass"
If you don't trust me with no pottery baby I don't
even know if we have any trust at all. I'm just saying
I have options.

I could always call up my ex
Don't even need call, could just text
It doesn't mean we have to have sex, y'know.

I might just go for a hike
The city's nice this time of night
Up in the hills, take in the sights.

I could always go to the gym
Not quite sure where it is, or if they'd let me in
But I'm pretty sure I'm still paying for a membership.

Or

I could just stay home

Few bottles of wine alone

Enough weed to get Willie stoned.

(Well probably not that much, definitely not that much, there's budgets when you're broke and no one cares if I sell Taco Bell, but I thought the rhyme worked pretty well y'know. I was only saying I have options).

BOXER

You had a few fights, not too many wins

You could have been a journeyman

You were in a bout they shouldn't have put you in

Eye permanently closed, the end of the beginning

Roaming the streets, till you started working in the gym

They started letting you sleep in the ring

'Cos man, those streets are unforgiving

You could always find your feet, my friend
You always could make everyone laugh, my friend.

For hours, we'd just sit outside, that place on Vine

Man, yours were the most interesting stories I could find

You always had a smart-ass comment for every passer by

They usually saw the funny side

Your intentions were never unkind.

Half a Reese's and a pool of blood was the only sign

You left behind, as you walked yourself to a friend of mine

He said you didn't look well, then I heard you kinda smiled

Before you told him, you'd been stabbed multiple times.

You told the paramedic she was pretty fine

Even asked for her number as you were about to flatline.

I tried to see you in hospital my friend.
But it's hard to locate an attempted murder victim,
harder still if the victim has no insurance and even more
difficult if you gave them a fake name, my friend.

A few days later you surfaced again

A tougher man there has never been

Remember at the coffee shop when that dude burst in?

He was twice your size, saw some people
he was harassing.

Next thing he knew, after swinging at you and you
hitting him

with a quick one-two he was on the ground wondering

what to do, all of a sudden he wasn't too threatening.

Said he'd come back when you weren't with your friends

You said "well shit, we'll just go for a walk then."

Heard you've been doing okay up North my friend
I look forward to hearing stories soon my friend.

OH SWEET JENNIFER

Oh sweet Jennifer
I hope you're sleeping tight
I don't expect a reply
It must be the middle of the night
In old Los Angeles
I hope he's holding you right
I'm sitting in this Yorkshire rain
My heart's heavier than it is light
Thinking about what I missed.

Oh Sweet Jennifer
If I do ever see you again
I don't know if I'd have a lot to say
Maybe I'd ask you if everything worked out okay
I was trying to do the right thing
But I have no idea what that is today
Maybe everything would be different
Or maybe it would be exactly the same.

Oh sweet Jennifer
They say there's a difference between love and lust
I don't know much
But there's over five thousand miles between us
Yet it's closer than I've felt to anyone in a while.
Oh sweet Jennifer
Don't forget to smile
Smiles get lost when the truth is found
So don't give that truth to the first person that's around
I'd give you the world
But I only ever gave you my pain

You wanted to be my girl
But I couldn't unshackle those chains
Oh sweet Jennifer
I hope you're sleeping tight
And I hope he's keeping you warm tonight.

RED, RED WINE

Drinking red, red wine, trying to unwind
Watched 'A Woman Under the Influence'
It was quite intense
Cassavetes
The older one, not the younger one
Peter Falk, Geena Rowlands, ooh wee

Drinking red, red wine starting to feel fine
Second bottle and I'm clearly under the influence
A Cabernet, quite intense
It was older than I could afford, but younger than you want
Smokey, peppery, wood, earth and all that shit.

Drinking red, red wine, starting to lose all sense of time
Listening to those Ramblin' Jack albums Guthrie influenced
Third bottle, rolling this smoke is quite intense
The night's growing old, but still seems young
Stumbling and mumbling to light this goddamn cigarette.

Drinking red, red wine, making myself blind
On my fourth bottle, I don't need no bad fucking influence
Blah, blah fucking words some more words then
the word intense
Tomorrow I'll feel old but tonight I'll feel young
Fuck tomorrow, four bottles of wine and I'm done.

I GUESS THE LIGHTS WENT OUT IN SOLANA BEACH

You tried to hide the obvious, but you drew me a map
I needed to seem oblivious, and I've always
known how to act
Baby, this all may be make believe, second chances
are hard to come by
This is our fifth or sixth, that doesn't feel like reality,
I guess we had to at least try.
They didn't say this was going to be breezy,
but I wasn't expecting it to be this hard
I suppose nothing good comes easy, I guess,
I didn't want to see us grow apart
Let's not be sad it wasn't all bad there was good times,
Solana beach when out went the lights
That shit was a trip, baby we got so high, walked the
railroad tracks, we had to stay an extra night
I guess we were past our laughs, occasionally we hid,
I guess we only ever pulled the wool over our own eyes
I guess the best must rest, no-one else to kid,
I guess we at least had to try.

WHITE RUSSIAN TABLE

It was July 4th weekend
My lady was playing some shows up in Oregon
She needed to spend some quality time with her friend
I had one week alone
I could have spent it at home
But I decided too, to hit the road
I had a friend with a truck
Just needed to get him on the hook
But luckily for me, he was feeling his luck
It didn't take much to persuade us
And little did I know, I was about to become
slightly famous
As I'd soon be part of the White Russian Table in Vegas.

There was no AC in his car
But from LA the drive's not too far
Still I was ready for whichever bar
Gas was running a little low
So, we pulled into a station at Barstow
Back on the 15 and away we'd go
When it comes to Vegas there's a lot of shit people say
Like, four days is too long to stay
But we were checking in for the week at the Mandalay Bay
That's where the White Russian Table was officially
formed y'know.

We checked into our rooms
It was safe to assume
That our leashes were off and we were certainly doomed
Smoking bowls in the shower
A few beers in the first hour

We were ready for the Strip, pyramids, gondolas,
volcanoes and the Eiffel Tower
It was the same every night
We'd drink till sunlight
Or till our thoughts were out of sight
It is Las Vegas after all.
The city of sin
Where to begin
This certainly wasn't the first time I'd been
My friend wasn't much into gambling
But agreed like all things it needed sampling
Even if it was just to stop me rambling
He won a couple of hundred on some roulette, first timer,
beginners luck, hit the double zeros.

Now, it was the last night of the trip
My friend was in bed by twelve, ain't that some shit?
So, I wandered around for a bit
Found a wall outside the Bellagio to sit
A perfect seat to see the water, which was lit
Then I wandered around the rest of the Strip
Blew a few bucks in the MGM, but it was worth the hit
That's when I slowly made my way
Back to the Mandalay Bay
Saw a half full blackjack table that looked okay
I kind of recognized the croupier
I sat down just to play
Didn't care if I gave my money away
Drinks are free at the table so I decided to stay
After all, twenty-one was always my game
Like always it seemed to start the same
A couple of wins to my name

Before I lose it and only have myself to blame
These guys sat down and I wanted to order a beer
But it became abundantly clear
The waitress had disappeared
Not me or any of the other guys could see her
To my left, at the far end
Was a happy couple, well, they were at least
trying to pretend
Right next to them
Was a girl with her friend
But they left the scene
At about a quarter to three
The table was left to me
And these new guys that seemed friendly
Three of them in total
All were staying in the same hotel
Turns out they were tired of waiting and sent their friend
for a bottle
Before the waitress came back
They'd passed me their bottle of Jack
This could change the luck I've lacked
We soon became friends
And started betting again
Turned out they were all Alaskan fishermen
The waitress came over
She tried to take our order
But before anyone else caught her
My new main man asked if they did White Russians
It turned out they did
So, he said "Listen to me kid,
Just because it's free and I'm able
I'm getting White Russians for the Goddamn table"

In fact, we had two each
And a beer a piece
This carried on as we played
People around us starting to fade
But me and my new friend Wade
Were content to drink and gamble the time away
The dealers rotated
We were joyous, jubilant and frustrated
But not once, was leaving ever debated
The pit boss arrived
Said she was checking to see if we were still alive
She knew we had much further to dive
Saying "I heard this was the 'fun' table"
Looking at our drinks she said "It's true, you really are the White Russian Table"
She checked on us throughout the night
Always smiling, always polite
But the time had come and I was out of chips
But Wade told my dumbass to sit
Said "Kid, if I've got chips, you've got chips"
It didn't matter that I'd just met this man
He said "We're the White Russian Table
we gamble till we can"
So, I was dealt a new hand
A win I would land
And no payment would he demand
But all of a sudden
His chips came to an end
But that was okay, I now had plenty to lend
Especially for my new friends
The Alaskan fishermen
aka Two thirds of the White Russian Table.

Some people may choose not to approve
But I've always abided the dude
"yeah, well, y'know, that's just like, err, your opinion man"

Musing #4

Lost in thought

Never thought I would

Always thought I could

They say, I never thought enough

But believe me, I thought too much

Who's to say, when they, think, they've, had enough.

I'LL KEEP ON TRYING *PREAMBLE*

I don't know if you have ever experienced this
And I'm not saying I have
I'm also not saying I haven't

But this next one is about that feeling
The feeling you get when you're trying to do
the right thing
But the ending often feels worse than the beginning

It's also about drinking and other things of that nature.

I'LL KEEP ON TRYING

I'm trying to go out tonight
Drink a few beers
Get a little crazy
Feel a bit freer
It is Friday night after all.

I'm trying to get drunk today
A few shots of whiskey
Get a little crazy
Feel a bit hazy (tomorrow, that is).
It is Saturday after all.

I'm trying to drink this hangover away
A few Bloody Marys
Get a little crazy
Go away with the fairies
It is Sunday morning after all.

I'm trying to forget my day at work
A bottle of red wine
Get a little crazy
Just trying to unwind
It is Monday night after all.

I'm trying to stay in tonight
But I got a call from some friends
Get a little crazy
We'll see how the night ends
It is Tuesday night after all.

I'm trying to be civil tonight
I got a date you see
Get a little crazy
Well, after she sees through me
It is Wednesday evening after all.

I'm trying to go wild tonight
After that date last night
Get a little crazy
She was not my type (I probably wasn't hers,
but that's alright).
It is Thursday night after all.

I'm trying to go out tonight
Drink a few beers
Get a little crazy
No excuses, I'm right back here
It is a Friday night after all.

YELLOW BIRD

You were a cheerleader from Texas
Out here following your dreams
Making out in the back of your car
We were only eighteen
But I was thinking about someone that barely knew me yet
So at best it seems
I can only wish to be, a memory you don't hope to forget.

You came from the Midwest but became a California girl
And I'll be the first to admit
That as much fun as we had, it maybe wasn't the healthiest
But we were working through a lot of our own shit
And I was certainly too caught up in my own
Drinking whiskey and smoking cigarettes
Company inside a bottle, I suppose, I was never alone.

I was attempting to fix my head
The first time that we met
You were so beautiful, kind and patient
But I wasn't ready to deserve you yet
I wish I could have told you the truth
But the truth wasn't something I was prepared to accept
The truth that I started loving you, but loving wasn't
something I was able to do.

We met on a rooftop at Columbia University
Wish I met you earlier because we only had a few days
Which probably helped me to not fuck up anything
too badly
But eventually you flew out to LA
Our dinner Christmas Eve, I must confess
I was a goddamn mess
Then you drove us to feed the homeless on Christmas Day
You were always so hopeful and true, not that I knew what
it is or was, I still knew, I was far from my best.

We grew close as we talked about our romantic failings
We ended up taking refuge in each other's arms
How could two broken pieces be expected
to fix themselves?
But we figured, trying wouldn't do any harm
You eventually wanted me to move into your place
And I couldn't explain to you with any sort of charm
That was a commitment, I was too scared to face, again.

My friend dragged me to her friend's house for this party
That's where I saw you smoking on the balcony
I couldn't wait to see you again
I wasn't lying when I said I was so happy
I just had no idea what that meant anymore
I wish I wasn't too blind at the time to see
That love doesn't have to leave just because
it's been lost before.

We met at work and you told me you were on
my side of town
Asked if I wanted a drink, which I did
It probably doesn't seem it to you
But I miss you laid in bed next to me, like the morning
we watched Butch Cassidy and the Sundance Kid
I must admit, I didn't know what the fuck I was doing.
Sure my emotions I always hid
But I just didn't know how to show you
something so ruined.

It's hard to ask for someone's love
When you don't know where love belongs
Sure, love is a gift that everyone seems to want
But I'm too confused to separate right and wrong
So I'll just keep rambling on, flirting with lady luck
I suppose Tanya Montana Coe said it best in her song
The song that says "ain't nobody gonna love me,
I'm all fucked up."

MY LOVESICK CONFUSION BLUES *PREAMBLE*

I wrote this next one,

Because I was in a state of confusion

It's about two people that feel like they should be together

But it is not practical.

For whatever reason

And the romantic within is trying to make it work.

It's also about,

A bunch of other shit.

MY LOVESICK CONFUSION BLUES OR I'M JUST TRYING TO MAKE THINGS CLEARER ON IF WE'LL WORK OUT, CONSIDERING MY SERIES OF FORMER ROMANTIC FAILINGS AND DETOURS

If one plus one is meant to make two
What would one think other than they already do?
I'm just on the brink baby, all this thinking about you
In fact, I'm turned inside out wondering what's true,
But, I guess if one plus one does indeed make two
That's exactly how I should feel about you.
Yet, I never was too good at math
In fact, I don't know if there were a test I passed.
What I lacked in smarts I made up for in ambition.
The same ambition that has me wishing,
It was you I was kissing, instead of out here fishing.
It ain't the city, the food, the people, it's you, I'm missing.
'Cos you know,
One plus one makes two, or at least it used to do
Though when I met you, I saw the number three
It was staring back at me.
What if one plus one actually made three?
Got me confused you see, who said that couldn't be?

What about two fives and a seven?
Does that make fourteen or eleven?

What if all the numbers actually meant something different in the first place? Hear me out darlin'

Like, if one was supposed to be two and two was supposed to be one, two plus two would be one, but then one plus one could never make two.
So, what the fuck are we supposed to do?

One plus one would make four,
But maybe four isn't even four anymore.
Maybe, four is five and five is four
But where the hell is three going to go?
Three is six and six is three.
Does that mean that sixty-three is now thirty-six?
Oh shit, I'll never get this fixed.

If one is two and two is one, three is six and four is five, six is three
It means everything's changed mathematically.

If one plus one is meant to make two
We can predict the outcome of one plus one

But if I take one plus one and turn it into four
We won't know what the fuck is going on anymore.

OLD FRIENDS

Old friends and old memories
I wonder how they'll remember me
I don't normally hang around too long
Before I'm leaving town, listening to a different song

I think of all of you often
I just never really softened
It's always been hard to find the time
To say what's been on my mind
But good and bad I thank you for
Even if I didn't become, who I could have been before
Too many stories to tell
Some sweet, some damning us all to hell

But every person I've ever met
Is a person a part of me will never forget.

RAMBLING #1

Sleep, they say. I'll do that when I'm dead.

When I'm dead, sleeping will be the last thing on my mind.

You'll find a sign of the times, is when the body groans.

Like a fucking medical show.

But there's no miracle cure in this episode.

This episode

Is real life.

In real life miracle cures are preserved for the rich.

I'm not trying to become political,

I just think it typical, how we lose ourselves,

living inside a map we drew for ourselves.

Maybe that's why it no longer helps.

We're lost in our own bad sense

I'm just rambling man.

GROCERY STORE BLUES

All I did, was step out to go to the store
I must admit, it is not my favorite chore
'Cos I normally get there and I don't know
what I want anymore
I'm not the kind of guy that fucks about with lists
I mean, that class on organization, was the one I missed
But if I can, please let me tell you this
I was on a mission that was quite serious
I was on my way to buy dinner ingredients
The door locked behind me, which is usually okay
But I had forgotten my keys that day
Had to call the landlady see what she'd say
Said she was going to be over right away
We all know that's just a thing they say
I was officially delayed.
Stepped onto the street guy walks into me
Out of politeness you know, I said "sorry",
to which he said I'd "better be"
Some people are just having a worse day than you,
I suppose
I don't know if that car honking is angry or
just seen someone they know
There's a dude with no shoes,
flipping off every car that passes
Shouting something about how they all need to
"watch their asses"
Everyone is staring down at their technology
Guy tries to hand me this brochure about scientology
Man, I'm just trying to get some groceries
Walk past this newsstand, check out the paper

Man, that shit is bound to frustrate you
We're killing each other out there, and
becoming desensitized
To everything happening in front of our eyes
Man, half these things are filled with lies
So much so, the things that are true we're sure
to not realize.
I hear people talking at the traffic light as I stand waiting
Everybody seems to be happiest when they're complaining
Sun is shining, they want it to be raining
Give them a drawing, they wanted a painting
Everything you love, they end up hating
I then got a call asking me to come into work
I said "I'm not trying to be a jerk
But I haven't had a day off and I'm going berserk"
People had shopping carts acting like it's a fairground ride
It was a goddamn circus inside
But the groceries I was determined to find.
I braved those stormy weathers
And gather all my shit together
I got broccoli, avocados, man all kinds of shit
I forgot to bring my bags that day
I tried to buy one, but they said that was not okay
They were out of bags and I didn't know what to say
Told me some story about a delivery mistake
Then when I said I have had all I can take
At the grocery store my groceries stayed
I don't need no dinner, the world is in decay
But it's alright, don't worry, I got a bottle of scotch and
my dealer's on his way.

MUSING #5

Some words are to be said
Some words are to be read

Some sights you're told to believe
Some sights you have to see

Some feelings you wish would stay
Some you wish would go away

Some love is meant to hold
Sometimes it's best to let go

Some thoughts are to be said
Some thoughts are best left in my own head.

COLORADO

First night we told the stories we thought we could tell
Meeting all the family by the fire while the snow fell
And boy, did it fall
Prompting us to make snowballs
Colder than I'd felt before
But breathing in that mountain air
I couldn't begin to care
We cleared the drives and away we rode
Into the mountains, we were set to go
The elk covered the hillside
I got as close as I dared try
We stopped by 'The Stanley'
Warmed up with some fine whiskey
The best we could find
Wasn't expecting my card to get declined
But you took care of the bill
Don't want to piss off 'The Shining' hotel
Made our way back to town
To see who was hanging around
Headed to the local bar
Drinking stouts by the jar
I know it was a few years ago
But I think of you fondly, dear Colorado.

OLD PHOTOGRAPHS #1

I'm sat here looking through old photographs

Some making me sad, some making me laugh

I know you have to leave the past in the past

But sometimes it can do you good to look back

Yes, the past is the past, but we all came from that

And ladies and gentlemen, that is a fact

We were laid on the grass, having some fun

My God, I didn't realize we were so young

I guess we can look at how far we have come

Now the pictures, I'm making my way through

And I find me another photograph of you.

This time, the years have moved on

And neither of us were looking so young

Your head on my shoulder but I see in our eyes, our song has been sung

I'm holding onto that picture, I don't know if I'll find another one

At least not a more recent one, but, shit, I suppose you never do know.

YE RUSTIC INN

I'd had one hell of a day
Not at all in a good way
Spent the day running around town
To find my friend, that had been gunned down
Chasing every lead to see where they led
Looking for my brother, laying in a hospital bed
I'd had no luck, when the darkness fell
So, to the local bar I went to dwell
Drank myself calm, whiskey, beer and gin
The features blurring at the Ye Rustic Inn
My friends were talking but I didn't care
I went outside for a cigarette and some air
That's when I noticed you, sat on the back of that jeep
Short denim shorts, tattoos, heavy eyeliner and locked
in a conversation that seemed pretty deep
Your friend went back to tending the bar
But you didn't make it in that far
You just stopped and stood opposite me
I still remember you staring so intently
As you asked me "Have you ever had a day where your
brain can't seem to handle it?"
I was thinking to myself… well… shit.
Said "I think I'm having one of those days right now"
It was like you knew somehow
You introduced yourself and I did the same
Girl, I'll never forget your name
I was still thinking about my friend,
I knew he was a fighter
You looked at me as you walked inside, saying
"It'll get brighter"

I said "Doesn't it always?"
Today has a beginning, middle and end, like all days.
I drank a few more down
Had a look to see if you were still around
But you were nowhere to be seen
Figured you were just a Ye Rustic mystery
But as I go for another smoke
I noticed you go for the door
You turned and smiled, said "Oh it's you"
You're like a fairytale baby, but I know you're true
You were halfway across the parking lot
When all of a sudden, your feet stopped
Your beauty paused the entire city
As you asked "Why's your day been so shitty?"
I said "Mine's a long story, you first"
I'd never seen it so peaceful over on Hillhurst
As you walked closer, you placed your hands on the railing, pulling yourself up
Eye to eye, into my soul you looked
You grabbed my shirt with your fist
Pulled me to you, so we could kiss
Then she let herself down and I can still hear the sound
Of her heels tapping against the ground
As she said "Hope that's made your day a little better"
I said "I can feel it turning around".

RUSSIAN GIRL *STORY*

Like most creative folk say at some point in
reference to their inspiration
I was going through a break up
I am not trying to show-off when I say
I am, no stranger to the break up
I have both broken up with people and
been broken up with
Neither are great
To be honest
Both suck
But, sometimes it just doesn't work out
And that's okay
But this break up was different to the others
This was my sixth break up
With the same girl
Sure, you'd think we'd learn after the third or fourth
But, no
We were on our sixth
Shit, I wish I could tell you that was the last time
we broke up
But, it was not.
However,
At the time
It all seemed pretty final.
We all have different ways of dealing with break ups
Some people eat ice cream
Some people head to the strip club
Some people hide inside
Some people work to keep busy
Some people download some dating thing on their phone

Some people drink booze and get stoned
On this particular occasion
I opted for the work and keep busy option
But as I was no longer exclusive
I also opted for the drunk and stoned option too
Quite the combination.
Luckily for me
At the time
My jobs were to tend bar
I worked a few shifts at this place on the eastside
The other place I worked
Was in Hollywood
Just off the Boulevard
Before you hit Sunset
Next to Cahuenga
Near to Vine
I still consider those guys my family
I was working long hours
But we always managed to make it out most nights
Drink till our shifts didn't happen
I'm not saying it is a healthy way to deal with a break up
But that's what I was doing
And that's what I did
Not that we ever needed any kind of excuse
I remember one time
It was New Year's Eve
We closed at one
But Hollywood on New Years'
Forget about it (read that line in whichever voice feels comfortable)
The streets were closed
And in Los Angeles

Nobody lives in walking distance
Don't feel bad for us
This wasn't our first rodeo
We had a few beers behind the bar
A bottle of bourbon
A bottle of tequila
And some moonshine
Not the fake moonshine
There was a band that played from time to time
They played that night
But one of the guys just came from home
With typical southern hospitality
He brought back some jars of the family moonshine
We had cards, dice, dominoes and dollar bills
The sun came up on us
January 1st
Sure it was New Years'
But we had nights like that on a fucking Tuesday too
Anyway,
This has nothing to do with the next piece
I'm just trying to paint a picture
Let's go back to my newly heartbroken self
I was the kind of blue
Where I couldn't taste food.
I dig food
But, shit my taste buds were depressed
Music only felt lost
Music is the one thing that has never failed me but I'd forgotten how to enjoy it
That's the kind of blue I'd been feeling
It was a Saturday
I had closed the previous Friday

We made our way to Piano Bar
Then caught the close at Outpost
Then ended up drinking on the rooftop
So, when I walked in Saturday
10 am
I had felt better
But I had a joint for me waiting
And away we went
It got to around six
And this girl walked in
Slightly taller than me
And I'm about six foot three
She looked like a model
She asked me for my opinion on a drink
I gave her some samples so she could think
It was pretty busy
We didn't have too much time to talk
And quite frankly
I'm the first to confess
My head was still up my ass
But she came back and ordered another drink
Asked when I got off
Just so happened that I was off around seven
That's when she asked me if I wanted to see a play
If you ever saw her
You would know
It's impossible to say no
But I really wasn't in the mood to see a play
Especially after the whole break up thing
But she promised me it was only sixty minutes long
Which it was
But she didn't mention drinks with the cast

False 'well dones'
And I'm glad I came along
But, after that was done
You said we'd have some fun
You took me to a couple of your watering holes
You reminded me
What music sounded like.

RUSSIAN GIRL

We drank a whiskey and cider

I couldn't think but to hide behind you

I got the drunken blues

Now listen to me

We'll absolutely see

The cider and the whiskey

Is affecting me

Now we're skipping bars

I'm lost in your arms

I'm so broken, I'm not even trying

You can share the cab I'm buying

Yes, we kissed my darling

Then I walked the rest of the way home

Listening to music on my headphones.

David Bowie, Life on Mars to be specific.

TREJO'S TACOS

I was loving life, I mean, we were a family
In the heart of Hollywood at District 13
We were a craft beer bar
Serving drinks local and from afar
Gourmet burgers and alligator dogs
Yes, we may have just been the cogs
But believe you and me
we were keeping the place alive you see
we'd close in the night but stay to play cards
we worked hard but boy, did we play hard
drinking our tips into the nights
throwing coasters and rolling dice
We worked our shifts and our regulars could choose it
Every bartender played their own music
As crazy as a shift would ever get
At the end, we'd all be shooting whiskey till we'd forget
That was probably the best job of my life you know
Then came along Danny fucking Trejo
Now, I'm not trying to be petty
I fucking love the guy from Machete
The owners wanted to sell, so he bought out my employer
Danny Trejo the ultimate badass destroyer
From San Quentin to Hollywood
Don't worry, I got another job and have been doing good
After District 13 had to go
Because of goddamn Trejo's Tacos.

I'VE BEEN TOLD

I've been told, I care too much
I've been told, I don't care enough
Lately, I've been feeling pretty rough
Maybe the late nights are getting to me,
Or maybe as I grow older, I look more carefully
At who it is I'm trying to be.

I've been told, my heart's so warm
That I have love to give all day long
I've never helped but to feel forlorn
There's a lot of other things I've been told
Like, with all the warmth comes incredible cold
So cold, a single look could break a person young or old,
or so I'm told.

I've been told, there's nothing but love in my eyes
I was also told, that caused the biggest surprise
To see none of it left, when we said our goodbyes
I know that love went somewhere
I'll find it, with no stone left unturned
I just have to care enough to get there.

'UNTITLED' IS THE TITLE OF THIS UNTITLED PIECE TITLED 'UNTITLED' *PREAMBLE*

I was sitting in on this lecture,
Guy was talking about this dude,
Went by the name of Immanuel Kant
Now I do not know if you have read Immanuel Kant,
He may have been on to some important shit
But that man, did not write to be understood
To be honest the translation seemed to be confused
But this lecturer man, he really seemed to care
He was excited, talking from the heart,
Kids were listening too
I mean, shit, some of them seemed to be enthused
I mean the students man,
They're all tapping on their keypads
Like they knew what the fuck was going on
But, I'd made a couple of cool drawings in my notepad,
So not all was lost.
It was nine am and,
well,
I hadn't exactly had an early night
the night before
but I was really trying to hear what he was saying
He started talking about every event having a cause
That's when I was no longer doodling in my notebook.
Instead I came up with this next piece
I'm not sure
I got out of the lecture what he intended me to
But, I was okay with it.

'UNTITLED' IS THE TITLE OF THIS UNTITLED PIECE TITLED 'UNTITLED'

A man one said "Every event has a cause."
This was met with a timid round of applause
He said "That applause was proof of a cause"
he explained that he thought that because
sound is made when you clap your hands,
that's just basic laws
like a break in speech creates a pause
when we said our vows, yours became mine
and mine became yours
That was at least until the divorce
but like I said before
Every event must have a cause, including
our divorce
you told me;
I put too much salt in the sauce
I don't close doors
seldom do chores
swore at my in-laws
and showed no remorse.
I suppose every event does have a cause.

A man once said "What goes up must come down"
Throw an apple in the air it will hit the ground
That's 'cos it went up, it must come down and
round and round.
If a tree falls down it makes a sound,
well I suppose that depends on who's around
You were my queen and you wore that crown
now I guess that's trash in a bag waiting to be found
we were once so high, I suppose we were

homeward bound
when we went from being up to coming on down.
you told me;
I act like a clown
And make you frown
Said I should drown
Or at least leave town
I suppose what goes up must come down.

FOR YOU. FROM ME.

There are many words I want to write for you
But none of them seem to do us justice
Besides, words can only be so blue
So, I may only write a thing or two
I know you took a lot of the blame
Sure, you deserved some, but I deserved the same
We were like pieces of a jigsaw puzzle in a charity shop
Only we belonged to a jigsaw in a different box
We could only paint ourselves so many times
But, hey, at least we tried
I want you to remember me at my best,
whatever that means to you
If he makes you happy, may you forever be true
Love never fades
It only ever changes shape
The past was never built to last and the future is
as bright as you want it to be
I really have to stop reading those fortune cookies
Sleep well, wake refreshed
And always remember, you've earned the best,
don't settle for less.

Your
Penguin.

DRUNK

I used to get fall over drunk
I still do sometimes
But that just reminds me
That I used to do that every night
Drink until I lost my sight.

I'm sat here sipping some wine
Thinking about all those times
All the times I drank myself blind
But I swear, I'm doing fine.

I used to get so damn drunk
I still do sometimes
But that just reminds me
Of sitting in those rooms
Drinking their coffee, inhaling those fumes.

You see, I always said
If I'd rather be dead
Then I'd drink again
Well, I've always been
A man of my word my friend.

I used to get wasted drunk
I still do sometimes
But that just reminds me
Of what it used to be like
Yeah it was fun, but I was a sorry sight.

I left the rooms in the past
Made some friendships I thought would last
Guess people just move on fast
I didn't prevent it turning to ash
Guess if I was an actor, I've been miscast.

I used to get stupid drunk
I still do sometimes
But that just reminds me
Of how bad I used to be
I'm glad I moved on eventually.

I was out here in the cold, as they say
Sometimes, I tried to drink my feelings away
But lately I've been doing okay
Finding different ways to get through the day.

I used to get blackout drunk
I still do sometimes
But that just reminds me
That I still like to get a little wild
Forget I'm grown and act like a child.

As crazy as I can sometimes be
I've checked out both sides of the boundaries
Turns out
I'm only free if I choose to be free
I don't know about that, but I read it on a fortune cookie.
(They have fortune cookies at this after hours spot,
good times).

SOMETIMES

Sometimes the stars shine
Sometimes the night's too heavy
Sometimes the ride's fine
Sometimes we breakdown in this old Chevy
Sometimes the water turns to wine
Sometimes it breaks the levees

Sometimes the moon glows
Sometimes behind the clouds, it takes cover
Sometimes her love shows
Sometimes she's someone else's lover
Sometimes the heart knows
Sometimes they belong to another

Sometimes the moon gleams
Sometimes its lost in the night
Sometimes we're on the same team
Sometimes it's like we choose to fight
Sometimes my smile beams
Sometimes it's a forgotten sight.

SITTING AT HOME, WRITING ALONE

I'm sitting at home

Writing alone

No telephone

No distractions

Me and my thoughts

No actions

When I sit at home

And write alone

I put some music on

Listen to this one song

A song about satisfaction

And its un-achievability

Don't ask me

Ask the Stones

Cos I'm sat at home

Writing alone

I need to change the tone

So I put this album on

Call it 'Scarecrow'

By this folk singer you see

The name you might know

John Craigie

He's pretty good.

He rambles too

You know that's what I like to do

When I'm sat at home

Writing all alone.

Listen to some rambling folk

Woody Guthrie

'Talking Columbia'

Willie Nelson

Sings about 'Maria'

Let's be clear

I'm just rambling on

To that one Dylan song

From 'Blonde on Blonde'

You know the one?

'Just like a woman' it's called

Todd Snider

Talking about KK Rider

Ramblin' Jack Elliot

Jerry Jeff Walker

And Townes Van Zandt

The list goes on

As I'm sat at home

Writing alone

Ramblin' on

With a head full of songs.

Sitting at home.

Writing alone.

HARLEM *STORY*

I was kind of, in between places.
One of my friends had moved out east,
He was over at Columbia University,
Said he had the summer free,
He also had a couch too.
That's enough for me, y'know.
So I went over to New York for a while
Man, I feel like we walked every inch of that city.
First night I found this bar in Harlem
Had a bar, pool table, shit,
What else do you need?
I walked in,
Skinny jeans,
Bracelets,
Rings,
Long hair,
Probably wearing some kind of eye make-up.
This did not seem like the establishment for such attire.
I used to play a lot of pool back then,
Still do,
But I also played a lot back then too.
So I threw a dollar on the table
And waited my turn to challenge.
The guy I played didn't speak to me until I beat him,
Then all of a sudden we became best friends,
So I started to get to know everyone that drank in there.
In the meantime, me and my buddy,
We went all over
Broadway, the Village, Chelsea Market, Coney Island,
Staten Island, all the tourist shit,

We drank in the bar Kerouac drank in,
we went to every gallery,
every museum,
shit,
I even met John McEnroe at a black tie event,
I was not informed that it was a black tie event,
nor was I particularly invited to it,
I may have looked out of place,
I didn't stay too long.
I'd always go back to Harlem.
They became a family over there.
My last night in the city
We all went to that bar,
As I was leaving just after 4am
One of the bouncers was sat in the backroom
I'd become friends with all the people that worked there
So I went to say goodnight.
He was a tough looking guy,
With scar all the way down one side of his face
He had a girl sat either side of him.
I said "thanks man, I've really enjoyed my time here."
He said "yo next time you're back home tell them you partied in Harlem and it's alright."
So I wrote this next piece
To tell everybody, I partied in Harlem,
Multiple times
And it's alright.
Harlem, this is for you.

HARLEM

It was late in the evening
Most people were sleeping
The drinks I was buying
When I made my way to old Patrick Ryan's.

I was looked after in Harlem.

The Apollo was on our left
When you played those guys at chess
We walked all the way from 125th and Broadway
All the way to 1st, today was a good day.

I was looked after in Harlem.

I was not too surprised
To see the area being gentrified
With Columbia students all landing
The projects tall and still standing.

I was looked after in Harlem.

I was told the times of the police rotation
In between, they'd head to the station
That was the time to buy
Anything you want to get high.

I was looked after in Harlem.

I was taught by a couple of tweekers
That you can tell the undercovers by their sneakers.
After I met you, we'd walk in Morningside Park
Before your work would have to start.

I was looked after in Harlem.

I was standing on a rooftop
Before you went back in, you stopped.
Said you had to get back to serving drinks
Gave me your cigarette to finish, tasted like mint.
Oh menthols baby. Always make me think about you,
still, to this very day.

I was looked after in Harlem.

You took me through your covers
Taught me to be a better lover
I still think about you most days
We took the train from Harlem, all the way out to JFK.

I was looked after in Harlem.

MR BARTENDER BLUES

"What's your lightest beer?"
I don't think you need to be here.

"What's your cheapest drink?"
There's a liquor store on the corner, I think.

"Can you turn the music down?"
It's your voice I'm trying to drown.

"Can you turn the music up?"
I've got a headache, you obnoxious fuck.

"Do you have a charger for my phone?"
I do, but not for you, I don't like your tone.

"What wine do you serve? I'm in a red phase"
It doesn't matter, they've all been open for days.

"What's your most alcoholic drink?"
If I served you that it'll end up in the sink.
If we're lucky that is.

"What do you recommend?"
I'm not your phone a friend.

"I don't want any ice in my cocktail."
I never thought my soul was for sale.

"Can I have salt and lime with my drink?"
You ordered whiskey, you prick.

I got the bartender blues.

27

2 more

1 law

4 paws

7 shores

6 doors

3 whores

5 times I've lost my mind, but what for?

They never made it to be.

DON'T SAVE ME

I hadn't eaten, wasn't really sleeping
I didn't know where to go
I'd been cheating and I'd been stealing
I was at an all-time low
But I stopped waiting for you to save me
Because I didn't want to be saved anymore.

Recently,
It's been seeming, I'm not really dreaming
What's ahead? I just don't know.
I got the feeling, I want to be leaving
Go back to that village sidewalk show.
But, I did stop caring if you saved me
Because I don't want to be saved anymore.

I've tried,
To do some healing, got me believing
That my shit is in tow
No deceiving just my mind I'm relieving
I'm ready to let you go
I stopped wanting you to save me
Because I don't want to be saved anymore.

GOOD LUCK BAR *PREAMBLE*

This next one
Is about a bar
A bar that was located a few blocks from a place I lived
Needless to say
I attended this bar on numerous occasions
With numerous people
This next piece
Is for Good Luck Bar
Good Luck Bar
Is one of those bars
You know the ones
Walk in sober
Impossible to walk out in the same state
Rumor has it
Like many places
In Los Angeles
They closed the doors
But for many years
She sat on Hollywood and Hillhurst.
Thanks
For never judging me
Always serving me
I never left that place
Without some sort of story to tell
And well,
There's many of those stories
that under sworn oath
a sworn oath taken by my brothers and sisters
and myself included
I can never divulge said stories

they must remain in the sacred chapel,
locked firmly within those old walls
That will now
probably be replaced with some new walls.
But I couldn't write this thing
Without at least
Ramblin' about some

Good Luck this is for you.

GOOD LUCK BAR

It was your birthday
And we were there to celebrate
Drank the night away
Headed back to mine, in quite the state.

You were visiting from home
We were there to admire from afar
She left me and you didn't know
They threw us out, for making out on the bar.

We were catching up
You told me he wasn't treating you right
We drank from that old cup
And I gave you a place to stay the night.

You moved your things into my place
Said you had to get out
That you didn't feel safe
We went to our favorite bar about.

Sat drinking Potent Potions with an old friend
I didn't want to speak, but words got away from me
I haven't seen you again
We just couldn't be what we needed to be (I guess).

I'd met you at Harvard and Stone
Which is kind of strange
It's not a place I usually go
But plans we arranged.

We got together over on Hillhurst
Ordered a beer, and a Fist of Fury
Whatever it took to clench our thirst
It was like you could see through me.

Into the night we fled
Tangled inside each other's words
Waking in your bed
In Hollywood's theatre of the absurd.

Me and my friends
Buying Double Happiness all night a long
Whiskey and beer holding on by a thread
Headed to a Thai place for some karaoke songs.

It had been awhile
But we had gotten back together
It was during our smiles
In between the stormy weather.

We walked down to good ol' Good Luck Bar
A place we'd been many times
We drank the menu, till too far was too far
Then we decided to gather all our dimes.

Picking songs on the jukebox
We had the thought that, people get drunk in bars, and never listen to the entire song
To combat this in our drunken logic
We decided, if we played the same song six times in a row
Maybe, just maybe,

Everyone would listen to the whole song
That's the move of two wily old foxes
Come listen to "One More Cup of Coffee" and sing along.

(We left during the third repeat on that "Your loyalty is not to me" line, all parties decided it was best for all involved that particular evening).

UNFINISHED

I can see your mouth moving
But the world around you spins
Is this a talk I want to begin?
For all the pain it'll bring.

I can still feel your breath
The morning's cold but it warms my chest
Your face is there when my eyes rest
At times, I couldn't love you less.

Take away my pain, I'll live on yours
The world seems full of closing doors
They say they must open but what's the cause
I hate your light but I love your flaws.

AGAIN AND AGAIN

I was standing on this mountain.
All had been forgotten
Talking to the wind
My voice was getting lost, it softened

Softened to say
That it was you that day
Walking away
Again and again.

Again and again.

I was walking by this coffin
Oh, it had been forgotten
Left sitting in a field.
People, they walk by here so often

So often to say
That it was you that day
Walking away
Again and again.

Again and again.

We stumbled across this fountain
Why was it forgotten?
There was no one in sight
We spent hours and nobody came

Nobody to say
That it was you that day
Walking away
Again and again

Again and again.

MUSING #3

I woke up today, got me thinking
I don't know if it's okay but I'd been drinking
Don't worry, I won't stay away, only if I start sinking.

Cos I've been running around for too long
But I've been humming around with this new song
It's fine for now, at least it seems like it's coming along.

I'm trying to remember this melody
But she's flying away from where she used to be
I was dying inside, with those memories slowly killing me.

But now it's starting to seem
That somehow, I'm getting over the fool I've been
At least I'm stepping out, I even sometimes
remember my dreams.

IF I WAS GOD FOR A DAY

If I was God for a day
I'd burn this motherfucker down and start again
If I was God for a day
I'd try to learn from my mistakes
If I was God for a day
I'd think, I only have myself to blame

They say, he works in mysterious ways
That's the caveat, that makes cancer in kids okay
Just like the earthquakes, volcanoes and hurricanes
Maybe the same reason famine, isn't prayed away
And why wars are fought and lives are lost all in his name
Maybe I'm blaspheming in part of some master plan, but even if I'm wrong, it still seems like a pretty sick game.

If I was God for a day
I'd wonder how such beauty could cause such pain
If I was God for a day
Every drought would be fixed with rain
If I was God for a day
I'd eradicate hate and release our chains

I'm not trying to offend
Nor do I have a message to send
Merely a perspective to lend
Because so often we tend
To get caught approaching the bend
But if it's God that you defend
Let the whole love, forgiveness and compassion parts stand out to you, because there's a lot of questionable shit,

that can make people act crazy, if you read the good book,
to the end.
Making everyone forced to pretend
That judgement awaits those waiting to amend
If I was God for a day
We'd all be fucking friends.

THE BLACK CAT

I needed somewhere to hide
So, I decided to step outside
The talking at the bar
Had been pushing me too far
Thought I'd have a cigarette
Figured that was the safest bet
I noticed you when I opened the door
You reminded me of a girl I used to adore
Your friend left to get another drink
That was when I saw those guys start to think
They could maybe go and sit with you
Which was exactly what one of them tried to do
But you told him he wasn't welcome there
The second he placed his hand on the chair
He turned and left you alone
Went back to his friends to groan
That's when you saw me standing
Noticed me smiling and understanding
You told me to grab my beer
Said to me "you can come and sit here"
I moved from where I came from
And we talked all night long
Staying exactly where we sat
On Sunset, sipping cocktails, outside The Black Cat.

MIDDLESBROUGH

It's been ten years since I left this place
Didn't know if I could even show my face
It's not every day
A smoggy lad jets off to LA
But away I went
And some time I spent
I've been in some Hollywood homes
I've eaten lobster, but I didn't pay y'know
Drove south to San Diego
Gambled up north in Reno
Sure, I consider myself part Angelino
But no matter where I go
Or no matter who I play
I'm always that boy from Middlesbrough
It may not be Beverly Hills
But, Beverly Hills, never gave me any thrills,
The Transporter Bridge, Bottle of Notes and the Boulevard
Roseberry Topping, average shopping and the Riverside
In 86 we did almost die
But we made our way from Ayresome Park
to the Riverside
One of the first of its kind
It's a town with flaws but a lot of pride
And most people couldn't be nicer if they tried
So, step into your local pub
And drink till they've had enough
I may have changed a little bit
But I've grown, dealing with a lot of shit
It wasn't no Pacific Palisades for me
Shit, I was sleeping on people's balconies

Yeah, I drank at the Chateau Marmont
But I also smoked a blunt out front
Now I'm not trying to annoy
I'm just trying to say, you can take the boy out of the Boro
but not the Boro out of the boy.

GOODBYE

I've said goodbye too many times before
I don't think I can say it anymore
So, I'll say "see you later"
Because baby, I can't make you,
Can't make you stay here anymore.

We were in New York at the airport,
A latte and a fruit pot is what you bought
Little did I know
That the fruit pot, you were about to throw
You said you didn't want me to go
I said "You know I don't live here right?"
But since I met you, I haven't slept at night
Thinking about you is just something I do, now
I've said goodbye too many times before
I don't think I can say it anymore.

I was travelling back to the UK
We were two grown ass men crying that day
We became brothers in a couple of months
Both trying to keep ourselves off drugs
It worked for a while, for both of us, I still got love.
For a while there, things got pretty rough
When you're trying to figure out, if too much is enough
That was a tough goodbye but I'd see you again
Then we'd end up sharing a beer my friend.

You stayed for about a week out here in LA
It was great, we spent every day.
Together, wandering around town.
My friend, all our worries were drowned
With all the alcohol we found
Taxi picked you up on Vermont
You tell me you don't want to be gone
That was a hard goodbye to say.
On Vermont Avenue that day.

I don't even remember the last time I saw your face
Was probably at that coffee place
Could have been the bar next door
Maybe it was outside the Comedy Store
I really couldn't tell you anymore
I just thought I'd see you again
Taken by the feeling, I miss you my friend.
Never got the chance to say goodbye
I don't like them anyway, so I suppose it'll be fine.
If you don't mind that is.

You came over to my apartment, said we had to talk.
We all know what that means, well,
you do if you've heard it before.
Said you needed to be alone
But I heard you earlier on the telephone
I wasn't trying to listen but my place isn't
that big you know
I hope he treats you well my friend,
I'm guessing this is where we end.

This is not something that I like to do
But my love, I think I finally have to say goodbye to you.

I didn't think they were going to take you away
I also didn't know you were selling drugs out of your place
You'll be out in a few years
Maybe we'll get the chance to share a few beers
But brother I won't be here,
You see I've been here for way too long
You know me, always ramblin' on
I have to move on from this place
Putting her in my rearview mirror today.

                      I've said goodbye too many times before
                      I don't think I can say it anymore
                      So, I'll say "see you later"
                      Because you can't make me
                      Stay somewhere I just can't be.

LAST SHEET OF PAPER

I'm running out of paper,
In fact, this is the last sheet
Which is frustrating
Because whatever I write will not live up to expectation.

The ink in my pen is low
There's holes in my words
Which is infuriating
For someone resisting this new generation.

I'm running out of thoughts
So much to write, but nothing I want to write about
Which has just got me waiting
Waiting so long I feel like I'm on vacation, a shit vacation.

There is nothing left
No more fucks left to give
I used the words frustrating, infuriating, and waiting
so I could write the word masturbating.
Yes, I'm too many years old.
I also wrote the words expectation, generation
and vacation just for some justification to
write the word ejaculation.

And that folks, is how I decided to use my
final piece of paper.

TALKING POEMS *OUTRO*

I didn't write any of this shit to sound smart
I told you that would be obvious at the start
I just wanted to talk
Talk to you
Talking's what I do
I sometimes get blue
But, shit, I warned you about that too.

They were my talking poems.

Occasionally they rhymed
Sometimes they didn't
Sometimes the rhymes were hidden
I tried to make each word the best
But, ultimately, I did manage to relieve some stress
That line kind of rhymed, but this one will be nowhere near
I guarantee you. So fuck, I did what I wanted.

I rambled at times
Probably wrote a few too many lines
But I was just saying what was on my mind
I did promise that treasure we would find
I don't know about that
But for you, I at least tried
I hope you didn't mind.

I just wanted to talk
Because talking's what I do
They were my talking poems
I hope they talked to you.

Blank Page

Blank Page
apart from the word Blank, and Page,
and apart, and from, and the,
and word, and and,
and 149

POSTAMBLE

THE IN BETWEEN PLACES, WALKING AROUND LOS ANGELES BLUES

i realize that all has come to an end
but I would feel like i failed as a ramblin' man
if i was not to ramble on
so, if you have some shit to do
or somewhere you need to be
maybe there is people, whom you need to see
then please
i don't wish to stop you
but, if you do have a minute or two
maybe more
i'll ramble on to you
if you don't mind, i'm going to share a thought or two
because i've met a lot of people
i could have met more
i could have met less
but it seems
it seems
to me
and i don't mean to be controversial
but it seems to me
that we all have our own priorities
we all have our own dreams
and we all have the idea of the people we want to be
i was in between places
i don't know, if you've ever been in between places before
it can be rough
but it can also be fun

time to time
i'd been giving a buddy a little cash
so i could crash
on his floor
stayed there awhile
but then i had somewhat of an altercation
with some gentlemen
and well these gentlemen were also involved
in a bunch of other altercations
only most of their altercations
were with a whole other group of people
those altercations stemmed from this group of people
wearing entirely different colors to the other group of people
so after my accidental altercation
which was a classic case of mistaken identity
thus leading
to me needing
to find another part of town to crash
had a friend living past Fairfax
said he was having a night in
watching a movie with his girlfriend
they lived together
i've crashed there a few times
he said he'd leave me the key
i may ramble
but where he left the key must remain a mystery
as i cannot in good conscience
share another person's key hiding place
anyway, he said as long as I came by
after midnight they'd be in bed
and the couch would be free

so i had, some time to kill
so i thought i'd head to the beach
walked up wilshire boulevard
hopped on the bus
at macarthur park
i could ramble about the bus for days
but the ride that day, was particularly uneventful
that was until
all of a sudden
without any warning
for some reason i will never understand to this day
a sixty plus year old woman
sat at the front of the bus
a sixty plus year old woman sitting at the front of the bus
tried to steal a skateboard off a kid
just tried to walk straight off the bus with it
he was holding it in his hands
she all of a sudden claimed it was hers
now i am not saying a sixty plus year old woman
cannot ride a skateboard
i'm not saying that at all
but if you saw her
you would see
she was not too steady on her feet
and all of that aside
this woman was still claiming the skateboard
was hers i mean,
i mean everyone on the bus saw
saw the boy get on the bus with the skateboard
but a bunch of people that were just getting on the bus
told the boy to give this woman her skateboard back
i could not believe my eyes

they just took her side
i was a few rows back
an' i was making my way to the front
she was old, white and fragile
he was young, black and still a child
a man stood up
before i got to the front
and he made sure
the kid kept his skateboard
i was just trying to get to the beach
i still don't know what she wanted with a skateboard
but i guess, we all want different things
i got off the bus near the promenade
third street
santa monica
used to work down there
so i knew a few people
but i just walked to the beach
walked back
went to a bookshop and sat
i was thinking about all kinds of things
mostly thinking of places i could crash
friends can be kind
but i never want to wear that kindness out
too much to think about
thought i'm in a bookshop
i'll pick up a book to read
there was one in arms reach of where i sat
in one of those comfy bookshop chairs
i opened up this book
and boy, did i relate
first paragraph read:

A light shines through a window where a curtain used to be it seems familiar but my head is desperately blurred. The carpet feels rough against my back and the noise of bottles clanking as I move my body into an upright position is an almost unbearable sound. I'm not alone. A sunken air mattress sits in the corner holding a man and a woman. The old beaten couch in the opposite corner is occupied by someone else. There's a crackle from a record that is still spinning and a painting hanging on the wall which my ex- wife left behind. I must be at home. I reach for a pack of Marlboro Reds, three cigarettes left, I pull one out of the pack to my lips, I reach in the back right pocket of my very tight black jeans to reveal a yellow lighter which some people may consider bad luck but I don't tend to worry about such superstitions anymore. I light the cigarette and let the smoke circulate around my head as I try to gather my thoughts. A shower might be a good idea but my ex took the shower curtain with her and that is not the only obstacle, a man is laid in my bath tub. There's no coffee in the kitchen and to be quite honest I'm overwhelmed that so many people can fit into this broken down, tiny studio in the middle of Los Angeles. All my clothes are packed in a bag by the door. I must be leaving. I pick up the bag and open the door, it slams shut behind me, it is 7am and I need coffee because quite frankly I feel fucking rough. As the door closes an eviction notice stares back at me in the face and this is the moment I realize I am never coming back.

book was called something
something about somewhere
could have been nowhere
but it was either somewhere or nowhere or now
i knew how he was feeling
with that eviction notice

but i guess everybody wants something else out of life
and that's okay
why does it matter anyway?
nowhere to be till twelve
killing time till then
maybe kill time a bit longer
it seems rude to get there too soon
i had things to do, the following day or two
but that day
i was just killing time
with whatever or whoever i could find
i step outside the bookshop
hear my friend playing saxophone
says we can get a coffee when he's done
he had plans to go play chess
but he wanted me to come along
so i waited around until he was done with his last song
we went to this coffee shop
i drank coffee
so did they
but they also played chess
now, i like chess
but these guys
i mean these guys
really liked chess
like for example
they had timers and shit
in fact, first time i played my friend
he beat me in four moves
ain't that some shit
i mean four
only four moves

but we played a few times since then
and i can't go on without mentioning
that one time
i was crashing on his couch a few years later
when he moved out to new york city
we took the ferry
out to staten island
we put the chess mat down on this table
he put his timer
on the side of the table it needed to be
and i proceeded to win
i'd like to tell you it happened again
but in all hundred twenty three games we played
he won the rest
but he was pretty good
anyway, back to the coffee shop the one in santa monica
not the one we briefly attended on staten island
but back to the current proceedings
in which i am killing time
and not playing chess
only spectating
i stayed an hour or so
thought i better go
i don't intend to be rude
but there's only so many checkmates you can see
and well, this too, may be controversial
but chess ain't exactly a spectator's sport
i thought about heading for the bus
but the sun was setting
and well, time was on my side
i didn't need to be on the eastside for a while
i didn't mind walking around

a little
sitting down
a little
and waiting on the sun to set
once again, she set in the west
so i took myself to the bus stop
took the 720 to be specific
720 is the number the bus
i do not know why
or if there even is a 719
but i took the 720 over to wilshire and vermont
then i took the redline
up to hollywood and vine
you meet all kinds of people on the redline
i'll tell you about it sometime
i walked over to meet my friend
in the pool hall above playboy liquor
i never could remember the name of the pool hall
it was kind of a hole in the wall
and i'm not talking about how the place is now
i'm speaking on
what it used to be
before it was bought out
now it's some fancy place for frat guys
and craft beer, all in bottles
all with those funky hipster labels
you know the kind
steve's beard beer from oregon organic and tastes like cedarwood
i'm just talking shit
but this place they charged you for everything
they took all of this place's character

like most things
i suppose, everyone wants something different
well before this joint turned into this other place
it was a little unsafe
but i always had a good time
i walked up the stairs
threw a few bucks down
that bought me the table for an hour
even got me a beer
rumor had it, pool wasn't the only thing they were selling
but man, that was just speculation
i personally did not
see, nor did i hear
anything
and if i did
hear or see
anything
i still wouldn't say shit
but my friend came in
a few moments after me
now ladies and gentlemen
my friend
my friend, she is,
by formal definition
what you may call
a badass chick
leather jackets, rock star hair and make up
and plays pool in her heels
when we met, she hadn't played much pool
but night and day
she played
with us

then she played with some other people and then she
played with us
and well, now, she's pretty damn good
and i always used to love
when guys would try to hit on her
then try to offer her a game of pool
she'd always say
she was cool
but normally these guys with a brain cell or two
would ask to play her for something like twenty bucks
and every time they tried to play their luck
i couldn't help but smile
as they'd leave looking like fools
wallets lighter
twenty dollars poorer
they only ever saw the heels
fuck 'em
we played a couple of hours
drank a few beers
said she was meeting her friends at the village
asked if i was coming
i said i might meet her later
wherever they end
it was a friend's birthday
he was drinking over at piano bar
thought i'd at least stop by
i was closer to some of his friends than him
but that was only because
up until then
we only met a few times
but he was one of the coolest dudes you'd choose to meet
you probably seen him in a couple of movies

but he ain't top billing
he's making a living
i get to piano bar
bouncer lets me skip the queue
they were at capacity
but it wasn't my first time at piano bar
it certainly wasn't my last
drinks were cheap
and sometimes free
we were drinking beers
shooting whiskey
live band
some blues rock
some zz top sounding stuff
but I found all my friends
where I'd normally find them
in the smoking area
and sure it's california
but that smoking area
well that smoking area in california
was smelling
particularly good
as it always did
i suppose everyone wants something
it might be what you want
it might be something else
now see
now see
i
i still had some time to kill
and it wasn't seeming too hard to do
even when

i said even when
you've got
the in between places, walking around los angeles blues.

got a call from my friend
the friend from the pool hall
telling me her and her friends
who are also my friends
were heading to the dark room
the dark room
off of melrose
said if i was ready to leave now
i could get a ride
one friend said she was staying sober enough to drive
by some stroke of luck
my friend's house
you remember my friend's house?
the one with the key
that i was waiting to go to sleep
his place was like six blocks
six blocks maybe seven from where
the dark room was located
so, i said i'd meet her outside
piano bar
but i was holding a joint
and i didn't want it to go to waste
so i gave the rest to the bouncer
that's why i don't usually wait in that queue
i hop in my friend's car
that's waiting outside
one seat left in the back
that seat, was for me

like most nights we closed down the bar
the bar on melrose this time
the sober driver decided to leave her car
because she would have no longer
been a sober driver
but just a driver
and given the state of intoxication
not a very effective one
everyone's splitting cabs
but i just need to walk
walk down melrose
everybody is now out of sight
the street is emptier than you will ever see
there was only me
only me i thought
that was until
i witnessed a coyote timidly crossing the street
not even a full block in front of me
now i've seen plenty of coyotes, up in the hills
but this coyote, had wandered some way
what was he doing?
why was he there?
i guess even coyotes can be on their own kind of kick
twelve had passed
sometime ago
it was sometime after three
i finally picked up that key
they were both fast asleep
i laid back on the couch
and finally closed my eyes
but i couldn't sleep
for thinking about the next place i'd sleep

but i was no stranger to this sort of situation
i've slept many places
beds, couches, chairs, floors, all kind of surfaces
but no matter what
i will never stop
and i will keep on a ramblin' on
it won't matter for me
winning no lottery
'cos i never minded
the in between places, walking around los angeles blues.